THE GUITAR
3 Chord Songbook

PLAY 50 GREAT SONGS WITH ONLY 3 EASY CHORDS

ME 2

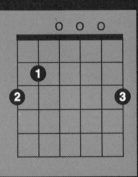

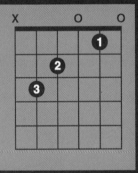

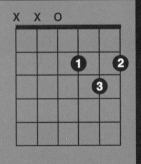

ISBN 978-1-4803-9969-3

HAL•LEONARD®
CORPORATION

7777 W. BLUEMOUND RD. P.O. BOX 13819 MILWAUKEE, WI 53213

Visit Hal Leonard Online at
www.halleonard.com

3 Chord Songbook

PLAY 50 GREAT SONGS WITH ONLY 3 EASY CHORDS

Contents

Ain't That a Shame

Words and Music by Antoine Domino and Dave Bartholomew

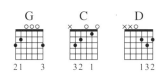

Verse
Moderately, in 2

1. You made me cry when you said _____ good - bye.

(3.) broke my heart when you said _____ we'll part.

Ain't that a

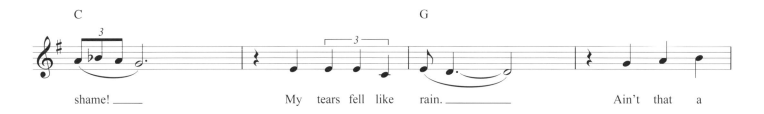

shame! _____ My tears fell like rain. _____ Ain't that a

shame! _____ You're the one to blame. 2., 4. Oh

Verse

well, good - bye, al - though I'll cry. Ain't that a shame! _____

My tears fell like rain. _____ Ain't that a shame! _____

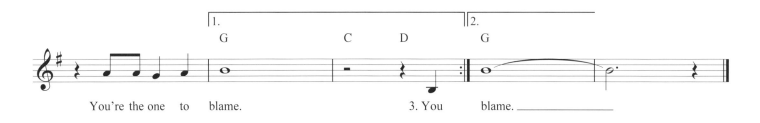

You're the one to blame. 3. You blame. _____

Cross Road Blues
(Crossroads)

Words and Music by Robert Johnson

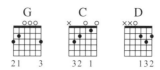

Verse

Moderately fast

1. I went down _____ to the cross - roads, fell down on my knee. _
(2.–4.) *See additional lyrics*

_ Down _____ to the cross - roads,

fell down on my knee. _____

Asked the Lord a - bove for mer - cy, "Take me if you please." _

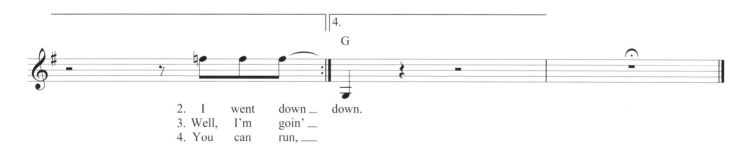

2. I went down _ down.
3. Well, I'm goin' _
4. You can run, _

Additional Lyrics

2. I went down to the crossroad, tried to flag a ride.
Down to the crossroad, tried to flag a ride.
Nobody seemed to know me. Ev'rybody passed me by.

3. Well, I'm goin' down to Rosedale, take my rider by my side.
Goin' down to Rosedale, take my rider by my side.
You can still barrelhouse, baby, on the riverside.

4. You can run, you can run. Tell my friend, boy, Willie Brown.
Run, you can run. Tell my friend, boy, Willie Brown.
And I'm standin' at the crossroad. Believe I'm sinkin' down.

Already Gone

Words and Music by Jack Tempchin and Robb Strandlund

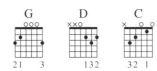

%. Verse

Moderately fast Rock

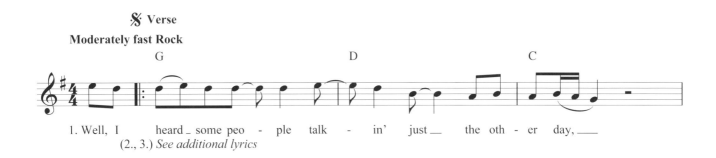

1. Well, I heard some peo - ple talk - in' just the oth - er day,
(2., 3.) *See additional lyrics*

and they said you were gon - na put me on a shelf.

But let me tell you, I got some news for you, and you'll soon

find out it's true, and then you'll have to eat your lunch

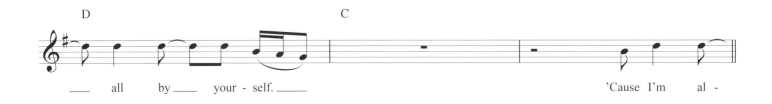

all by your - self. 'Cause I'm al -

Chorus

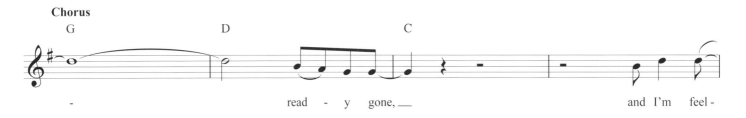

- read - y gone, and I'm feel -

in' strong. — I will sing ———

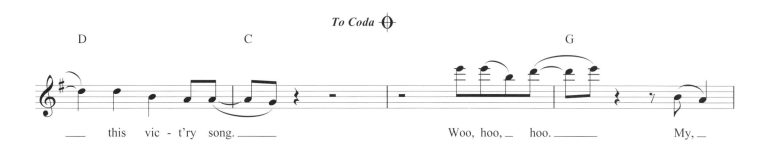

— this vic - t'ry song. ——— Woo, hoo, — hoo. ——— My, —

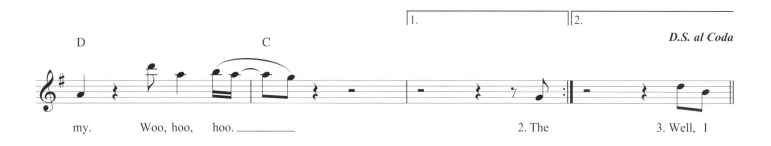

my. Woo, hoo, hoo. ——— 2. The 3. Well, I

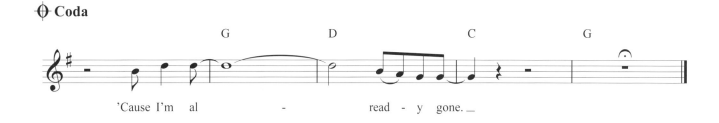

'Cause I'm al - read - y gone. —

Additional Lyrics

2. The letter that you wrote me made me stop and wonder why,
   But I guess you felt like you had to set things right.
   Just remember this, my girl, when you look up in the sky:
   You could see the stars and still not see the light. That's right.
   And I'm... *(To Chorus)*

3. Well, I know it wasn't you who held me down.
   Heaven knows it wasn't you who set me free.
   So often times it happens that we live our lives in chains,
   And we never even know we had the key.
   But me, I'm... *(To Chorus)*

Authority Song

Words and Music by John Mellencamp

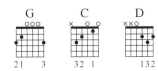

Verse
Moderately fast Rock

1. They ____ like to get you in a com - pro - mis - in' po - si - tion.
(2.) *See additional lyrics*

Yeah, they ____ like to get you there, ____ smile in your face. _____

Well, they think ____ they're so cute when they got you in that ____ con - di -

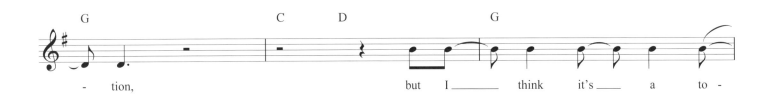

- tion, but I _____ think it's ____ a to -

- tal ____ dis - grace. _____ And ____ I say: ____ I ____

% Chorus

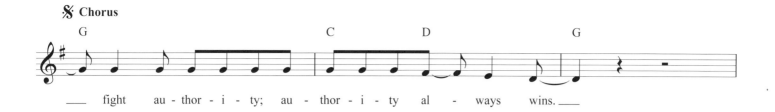

___ fight au-thor-i-ty; au-thor-i-ty al - ways wins. ___

Well, I ___ fight au-thor-i-ty; au-thor-i-ty al - ways wins. ___

Well, I been do-in' it since ___ I was a young kid, and I come out grin - nin'.

To Coda

Well, I ___ fight au-thor-i-ty; au-thor-i-ty al - ways wins. ___

D.S. al Coda   **Coda**

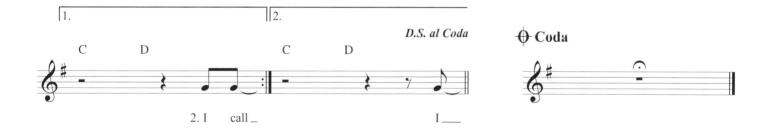

2. I call ___   I ___

Additional Lyrics

2. I call up my preacher. I say, "Give me strength for Round Five."
He said, "You don't need no strength. You need to grow up, son."
I say, "Growin' up leads to growin' old and then dyin'.
And dyin', to me, don't sound like all that much fun."
So I say:

Big Boss Man

Words and Music by Al Smith and Luther Dixon

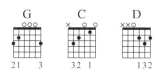

Chorus
Moderately slow, in 2

Big   boss   man,   can't   you   hear   me   when   I

call?   Big   boss   man,

can't   you   hear   me   when   I   call?

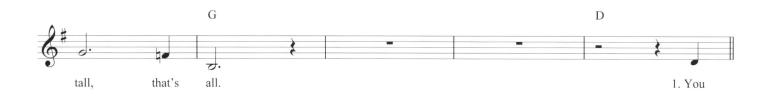

Well, ___ you   ain't   so   tall,   that's   all.   big, ___   you   just

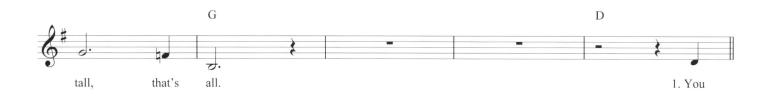

tall,   that's   all.   1. You

Verse

got me work - in', boss ___ man, work - in' 'round the clock. __ I
(2.) gon - na get me a boss man, one gon-na treat me right. __

want a lit - tle drink of wa - ter, but you won't let Jim - my stop. _____ Big boss
Work hard in the day - time, rest eas - y at night. __

Chorus

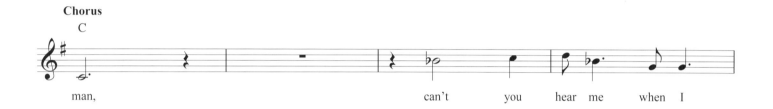

man, can't you hear me when I

call? Well, ___ you

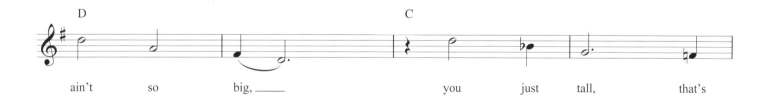

ain't so big, ___ you just tall, that's

all. 2. Well, I'm

11

Big Yellow Taxi

Words and Music by Joni Mitchell

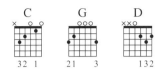

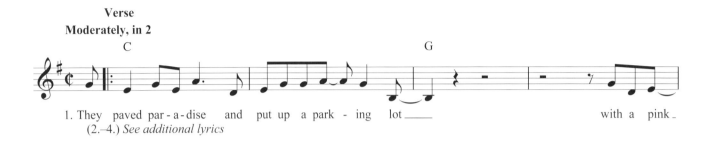

1. They paved par-a-dise and put up a park-ing lot ____ with a pink ____
(2.–4.) *See additional lyrics*

____ ho-tel, ____ a bou-tique and a swing - in' hot ____ spot. ____

Chorus

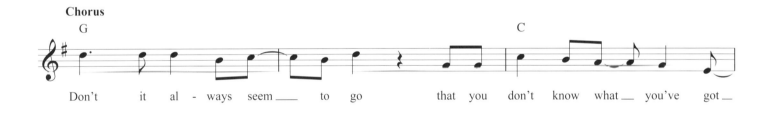

Don't it al - ways seem ____ to go that you don't know what ____ you've got ____

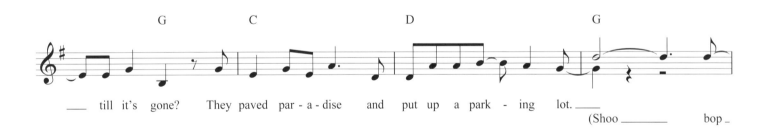

____ till it's gone? They paved par-a-dise and put up a park - ing lot. ____
(Shoo _____ bop ____

1.–3.   **4.**

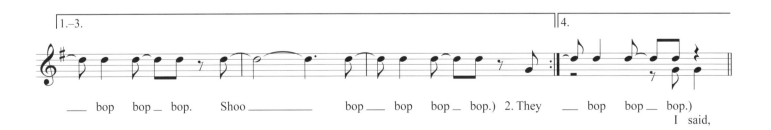

____ bop bop ____ bop. Shoo _____ bop ____ bop bop ____ bop.) 2. They ____ bop bop ____ bop.)
I said,

Outro-Chorus

don't it al - ways seem ___ to go   that you don't know what ___ you've got ___ till it's gone? They

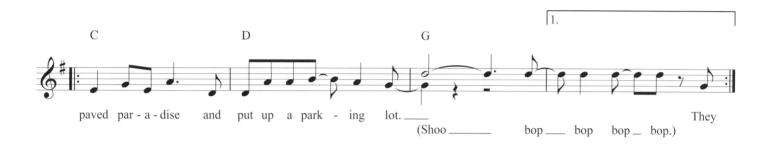

paved par - a - dise   and put up a park - ing lot. ___

(Shoo ___   bop ___ bop bop ___ bop.)   They

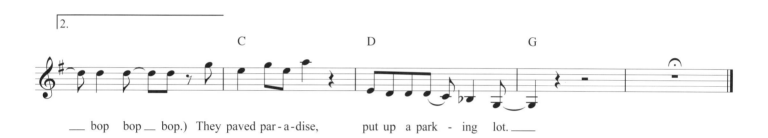

___ bop bop ___ bop.) They paved par - a - dise,   put up a park - ing lot. ___

Additional Lyrics

2. They took all the trees, put 'em in a tree museum,
   And they charged the people a dollar and a half just to see 'em.

3. Hey, farmer, farmer, put away that DDT now.
   Give me spots on my apples, but leave the birds and the bees, please.

4. Late last night, I heard the screen door slam,
   And a big, yellow taxi took away my old man.

Blue Eyes Crying in the Rain

Words and Music by Fred Rose

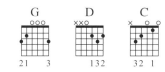

ag - es   I'll re - mem - ber   blue   eyes

D.C. al Coda

cry - in'   in the rain.

⊕ Coda

Outro-Chorus

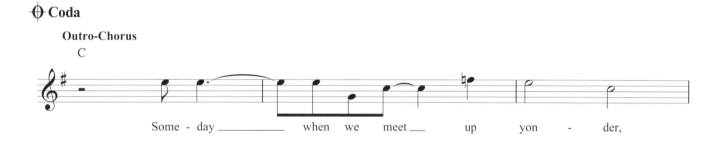

Some - day _____ when we meet __ up   yon - der,

we'll   stroll   hand   in hand   a - gain

in _____   a   land   that knows   no

part - ing,   blue   eyes

cry - in' _____ in the rain.

Blue Suede Shoes

Words and Music by Carl Lee Perkins

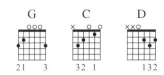

Verse
Bright Country Shuffle

1., 4. Well, it's one for the mon-ey, two for the show, three to get read-y, now

go, {cat, go,} go, but don't ___ you ___ step on my blue suede

shoes. Well, you can do an-y-thing ___ but lay

off of my blue ___ suede shoes. 2. Well, you can

Verse

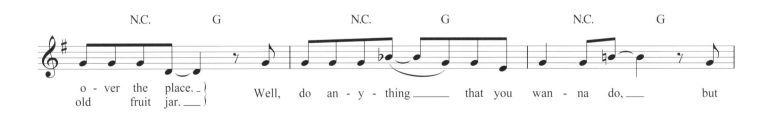

knock me down, ___ step in my face, ___ slan-der my name all
(3.) burn my house, ___ steal my car, ___ drink my li-quor from an

o-ver the place. } old fruit jar. } Well, do an-y-thing ___ that you wan-na do, ___ but

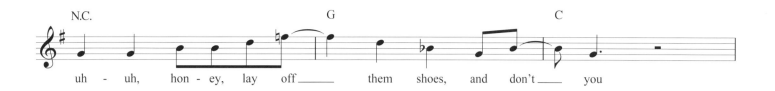

uh - uh, hon - ey, lay off___ them shoes, and don't ____ you

step on my blue suede shoes. Well, you can do an - y - thing, _ but lay

off of my blue ___ suede shoes. 3. Well, you can

4. Well, it's   Well, it's   blue,   blue,

blue suede shoes,   blue, blue,   blue suede shoes, yeah,   blue, blue,

blue suede shoes, ba - by,   blue, blue,   blue suede shoes. _ Well, you can

do an - y - thing _ but lay off ___ of my __ blue suede shoes.

Boom Boom

Words and Music by John Lee Hooker

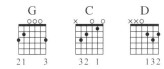

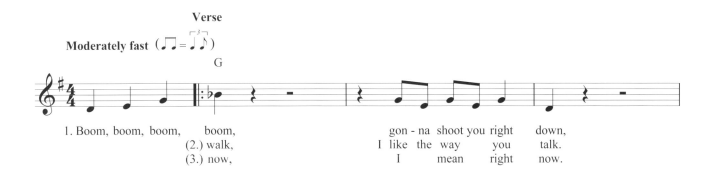

Verse

Moderately fast

1. Boom, boom, boom, boom,
(2.) walk,
(3.) now,

gon - na shoot you right down,
I like the way you talk.
I mean right now.

take you in my arms;
When you walk that walk
I don't mean to - mor-row,

I'm in love with
and you talk with the
I mean right

you.
talk,
now.

Love that is true, _____
you knock me out, _____
Come on, come on, _____

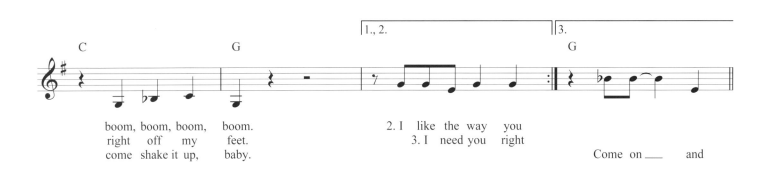

1., 2.

3.

boom, boom, boom, boom.
right off my feet.
come shake it up, baby.

2. I like the way you
3. I need you right

Come on _____ and

Chorus

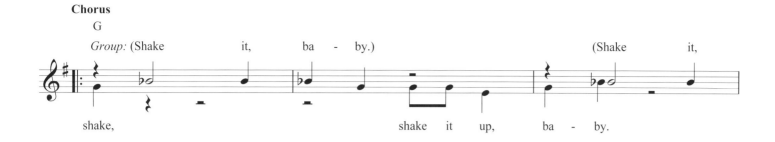

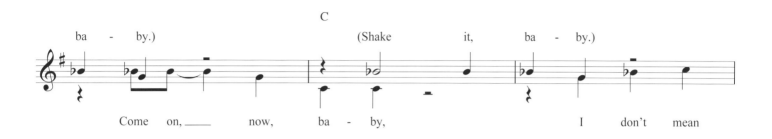

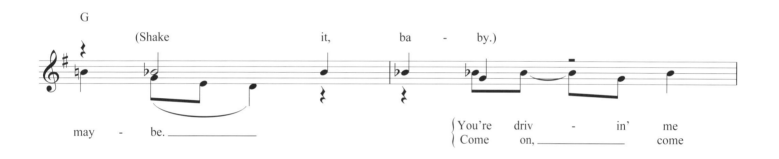

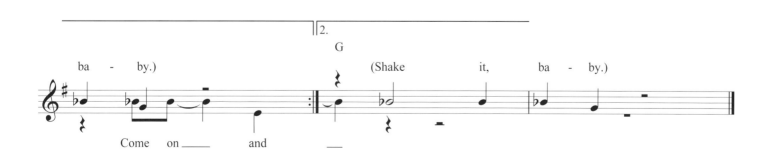

Boot Scootin' Boogie

Words and Music by Ronnie Dunn

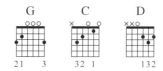

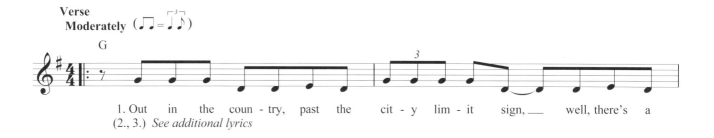

Verse
Moderately

1. Out in the coun - try, past the cit - y lim - it sign, ___ well, there's a
(2., 3.) *See additional lyrics*

hon - ky - tonk ___ near the coun - ty line. ___ The joint starts jump - in' ev - 'ry

night when the sun ___ goes down. ___ They got whis -

- key, wom - en, ___ mu - sic and smoke. ___ It's where all the cow - boy folk ___

___ go to boot scoot - in' boog - ie. ___

1.

2. I've

2., 3.

Yeah. ___

Heel to toe, do - si - do, come on, ba - by, let's go boot scoot - in'! Whoa, __

Cad - il - lac, Black - jack, ba - by, meet me out back. We're gon-na boog - ie.

Oh, __ get down, turn a - round, __ go to town, __ boot scoot - in' boog - ie. _____

1.
D.C.
(take 2nd ending)
3. The

2.
D.S. al Coda
Yeah. __

Coda
I ____ said,

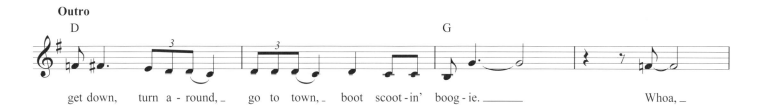

Outro

get down, turn a - round, __ go to town, __ boot scoot - in' boog - ie. _____ Whoa, __

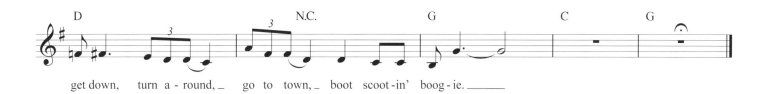

get down, turn a - round, __ go to town, __ boot scoot - in' boog - ie. _____

Additional Lyrics

2. I've got a good job, I work hard for my money.
   When it's quittin' time, I hit the door runnin'.
   I fire up my pickup truck and let the horses run.
   I go flyin' down that highway to that hideaway
   Stuck out in the woods, to do the boot scootin' boogie.

3. The bartender asks me, says, "Son, what will it be?"
   I want a shot at that red-head yonder lookin' at me.
   The dance floor's hoppin' and it's hotter than the Fourth of July.
   I see outlaws, in-laws, crooks and straights,
   All out makin' it shake, doin' the boot scootin' boogie.

Breakfast at Tiffany's

Words and Music by Todd Pipes

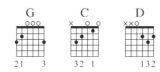

1. You'll say ___ we've got noth - ing in com - mon, no
(2.) see you, ___ the on - ly one ___ who knew ___ me, but
3. You'll say ___ that we've got noth - ing in com - mon, no

com - mon ground ___ to start ___ from, and we're fall - ing ___ a - part. ___
now your eyes ___ see through ___ me. I guess I ___ was wrong.
com - mon ground ___ to start ___ from, and we're fall - ing ___ a - part. ___

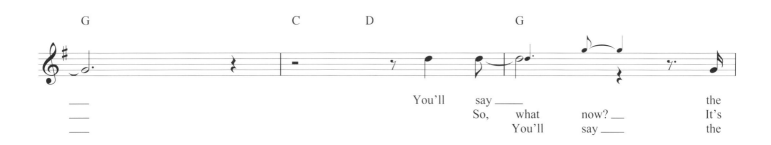

___ You'll say ___ the
___ So, what now? ___ It's
___ You'll say ___ the

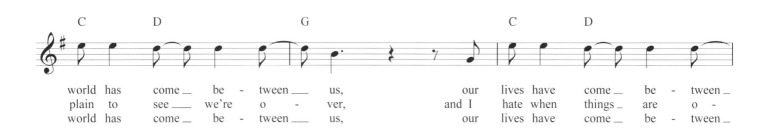

world has come ___ be - tween ___ us, our lives have come ___ be - tween ___
plain to see ___ we're o - ver, and I hate when things ___ are o -
world has come ___ be - tween ___ us, our lives have come ___ be - tween ___

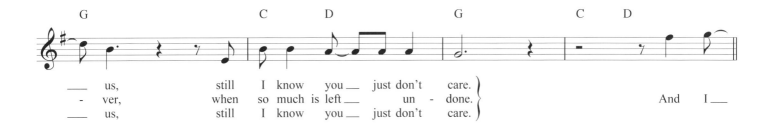

_____ us, still I know you __ just don't care.
- ver, when so much is left __ un - done.
_____ us, still I know you __ just don't care.

And I __

Chorus

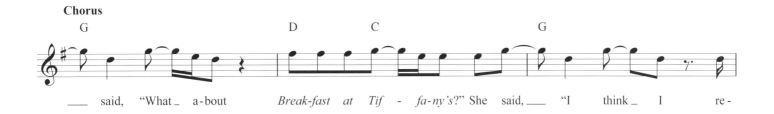

_____ said, "What _ a-bout _Break-fast at Tif - fa-ny's?_" She said, ___ "I think _ I re -

mem-ber the film, __ and as I re - call, _ I ___ think we both kind - a liked _ it." ___ And I __

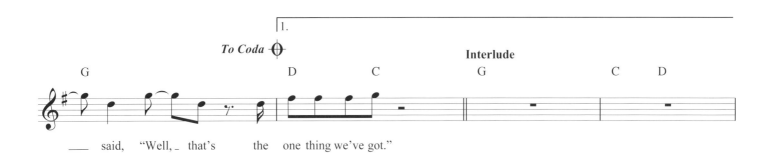

1.

To Coda ⊕

Interlude

_____ said, "Well, _ that's the one thing we've got."

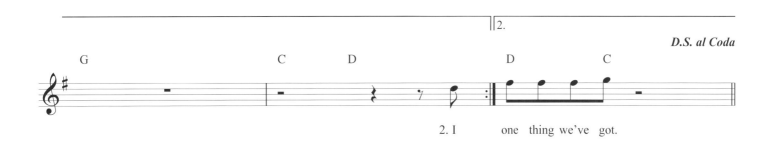

2.

D.S. al Coda

2. I one thing we've got.

⊕ **Coda**

one thing we've got.

Cherry, Cherry

Words and Music by Neil Diamond

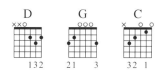

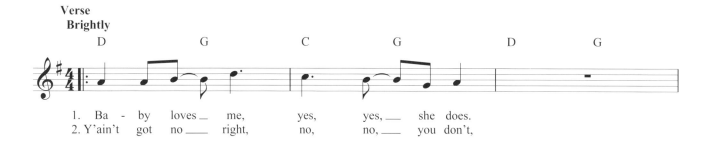

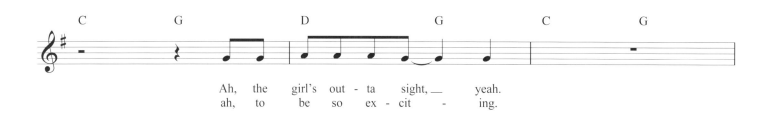

Verse
Brightly

1. Ba - by loves __ me, yes, yes, __ she does.
2. Y'ain't got no __ right, no, no, __ you don't,

Ah, the girl's out - ta sight, __ yeah.
ah, to be so ex - cit - ing.

Says she loves __ me, yes, yes, __ she does.
Won't need bright __ lights, no, no, __ we won't.

Gon - na show me to - night, __ yeah.
Gon - na make our own light - ning.

Chorus

She got the way to move __ me, Cher - ry. She got the way to groove __ me.

She got the way to move __ me, Cher - ry. She got the way to groove __ me.

Bridge

Tell your ma - ma, girl, __ I can't stay long.
No, we won't __ tell a soul __ where we gone __ to.

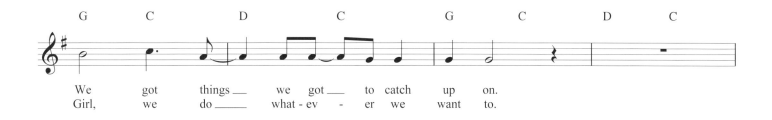

We got things __ we got __ to catch up on.
Girl, we do _____ what - ev - er we want to.

Ah, you know, __ you know __ what I'm say - ing.
Ah, I love ____ the way __ that you do me.

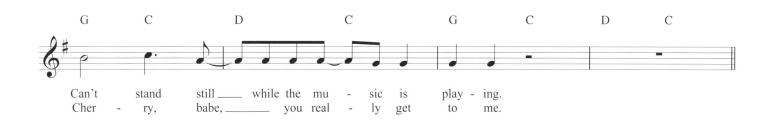

Can't stand still ____ while the mu - sic is play - ing.
Cher - ry, babe, _____ you real - ly get to me.

Interlude

2nd time, D.S. al Fine

Coat of Many Colors

Words and Music by Dolly Parton

Verse
Moderately, in 2

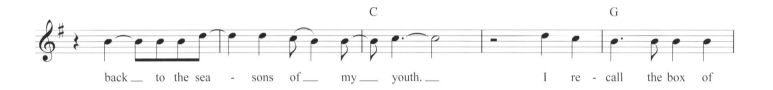

1. Back through the years ___ I go wan - d'ring once a - gain, ___

back ___ to the sea - sons of ___ my ___ youth. ___ I re - call the box of

rags ___ that some-one gave us and how my ma-ma put the rags ___ to use.

Verse

2. There were ___ rags of man - y col - ors, ___ but ev - 'ry piece was small, and I
(3.–5.) *See additional lyrics*

did-n't have a coat ___ and it was way down in the fall. ___ Ma-ma sewed the rags to-

geth-er, sew-in' ev - 'ry piece with love. ___ She made my coat of man-y col - ors ___ that

I was so proud of._____ 3. As she ___ My coat of man-y col-ors that my
5. And, ___ But they did-n't un-der - stand it, and I

ma-ma made for me, made on - ly from rags, but I wore it so proud - ly.
tried to make them see that one is on - ly poor on - ly if they choose to be.

Al - though we had __ no mon-ey, well, I was rich as I____ could be
Now, I know we had __ no mon-ey, but I was rich as I____ could be

To Coda ⊕

__ in my coat of man - y col - ors_____ my ma-ma made _ for me.

D.S. al Coda
(with repeat)

⊕ **Coda**

4. So, with me, _____ made just for me. _____

Additional Lyrics

3. As she sewed, she told a story
   From the Bible she had read,
   About a coat of many colors
   Joseph wore, and then she said,
   "Perhaps this coat will bring you
   Good luck and happiness."
   And I just couldn't wait to wear it,
   And Mama blessed it with a kiss.

4. So, with patches on my britches
   And holes in both my shoes,
   In my coat of many colors
   I hurried off to school,
   Just to find the others laughin'
   And makin' fun of me
   In my coat of many colors
   My mama made for me.

5. And, oh, I couldn't understand it,
   For I felt I was rich,
   And I told 'em of the love
   My mama sewed in ev'ry stitch.
   And I told them all the story
   Mama told me while she sewed,
   And how my coat of many colors
   Was worth more than all their clothes.

Cryin' Time

Words and Music by Buck Owens

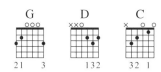

Additional Lyrics

2. Now, you said that you've found someone you love better.
   That's the way it's happened ev'ry time before.
   And as sure as the sun comes up tomorrow,
   Cryin' time will start when you walk out the door.

Da Doo Ron Ron
(When He Walked Me Home)

Words and Music by Ellie Greenwich, Jeff Barry and Phil Spector

Additional Lyrics

2. He knew what he was doin' when he caught my eye.
Da doo ron ron ron, da doo ron ron.
He looked so quiet, but my, oh, my.
Da doo ron ron ron, da doo ron ron.

Chorus: Yes, he caught my eye. Yes, my, oh, my.
And when he walked me home,
Da doo ron ron ron, da doo ron ron.

3. He picked me up at seven and he looked so fine.
Da doo ron ron ron, da doo ron ron.
Someday soon I'm gonna make him mine.
Da doo ron ron ron, da doo ron ron.

Chorus: Yes, he looked so fine. Yes, I'll make him mine.
And when he walked me home,
Da doo ron ron ron, da doo ron ron.

Dixie Chicken

Words and Music by Lowell George and Martin Kibbee

Additional Lyrics

3. Well, well, it's been a year since she ran away.
   Guess that guitar player sure could play.
   She always liked to sing along,
   She always handy with a song.
   Then one night in the lobby, yeah, of the Commodore Hotel,
   I chanced to meet a bartender who said he knew her well.
   And as he handed me a drink, he began to hum a song,
   And all the boys there at the bar began to sing along.

Elvira

Words and Music by Dallas Frazier

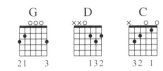

Chorus
Moderate Country beat

El - vi - ra, El - vi - ra, my

heart's on fire for El - vi - ra.

Verse

1. Eyes that look like heav - en, lips like cher - ry wine. That
(2.) night I'm gon - na meet her at the Hun - gry House Ca - fé, and

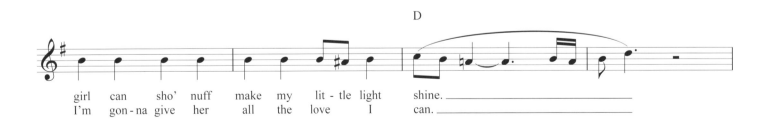

girl can sho' nuff make my lit - tle light shine. _____
I'm gon - na give her all the love I can. _____

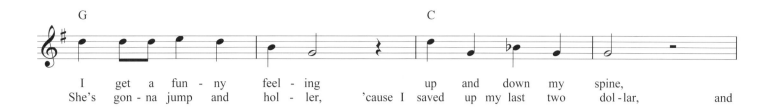

I get a fun - ny feel - ing up and down my spine,
She's gon - na jump and hol - ler, 'cause I saved up my last two dol - lar, and

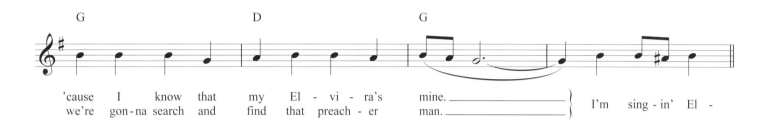

'cause I know that my El - vi - ra's mine. _____ I'm sing - in' El -
we're gon - na search and find that preach - er man. _____

𝄋 Chorus

vi - ra, El - vi - ra, my heart's on

Bridge

fi - re for El - vi - ra. Gid - dy - up, a - oom - pa - pa

oom - pa - pa mow mow. Gid - dy - up, a - oom - pa - pa oom - pa - pa mow mow. Hi - yo

|1. |2.   *D.S. and fade*

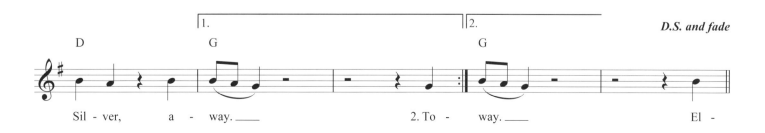

Sil - ver, a - way. _____ 2. To - way. _____ El -

Folsom Prison Blues

Words and Music by John R. Cash

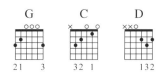

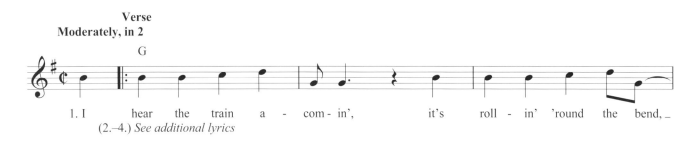

Verse
Moderately, in 2

1. I hear the train a - com - in', it's roll - in' 'round the bend, _
(2.–4.) *See additional lyrics*

_ and I ain't seen the sun - shine since I don't _ know when. I'm

stuck in Fol - som Pris - on and time keeps drag - gin' on. _

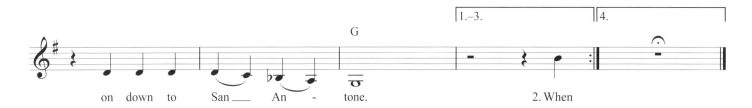

But that train keeps a - roll - in'

on down to San _ An - tone. 2. When

Additional Lyrics

2. When I was just a baby, my mama told me, "Son,
Always be a good boy; don't ever play with guns."
But I shot a man in Reno, just to watch him die.
When I hear that whistle blowin', I hang my head and cry.

3. I bet there's rich folks eatin' in a fancy dining car.
They're prob'ly drinkin' coffee and smokin' big cigars.
Well, I know I had it comin', I know I can't be free.
But those people keep a-movin' and that's what tortures me.

4. Well, if they freed me from this prison, if that railroad train was mine,
I bet I'd move it on a little farther down the line.
Far from Folsom Prison, that's where I want to stay.
And I'd let that lonesome whistle blow my blues away.

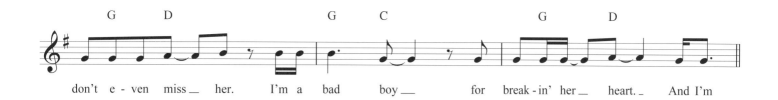
don't e - ven miss __ her. I'm a bad boy __ for break - in' her __ heart. __ And I'm

Chorus

free, free fall - in'. Yeah, I'm free,

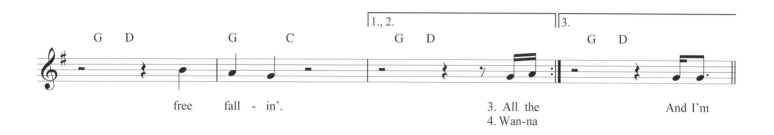
free fall - in'.

3. All the
4. Wan-na

And I'm

Outro-Chorus

Repeat and fade

free, free fall - in'. Yeah, I'm

Additional Lyrics

3. All the vampires walkin' through the valley
   Move west down Ventura Boulevard.
   And all the bad boys are standin' in the shadows,
   And the good girls are home with broken hearts.

4. Wanna glide down over Mulholland.
   I wanna write her name in the sky.
   I wanna free fall out into nothin'.
   Gonna leave this world for a while.

The Gambler

Words and Music by Don Schlitz

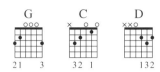

Verse

Moderately, in 2

1. On a warm sum-mer's eve-nin', on a train bound for no-
(2.–5.) *See additional lyrics*

- where, I met up with a gam-bler; we were

both too tired to sleep. ___ So, we took turns ___ a-star-in' out the

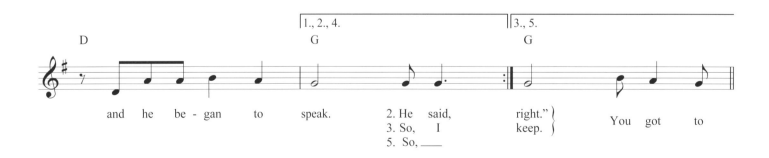

win-dow at the dark-ness till bore-dom o-ver-took ___ us,

1., 2., 4. **3., 5.**

D G G

and he be-gan to speak. 2. He said, right." You got to
3. So, I keep.
5. So, ___

Chorus

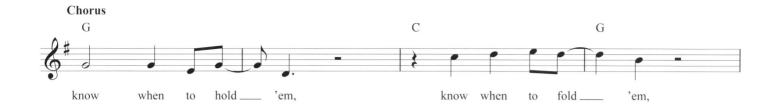

know when to hold ____ 'em, know when to fold ____ 'em,

know when to walk ____ a - way ____ and know when to run. ____ You nev - er

count your mon-ey when you're sit-tin' at the ta - ble. There'll be time e - nough ____ for count-

To Coda ⊕   ***D.S. al Coda***   ⊕ **Coda**
   (with repeat)

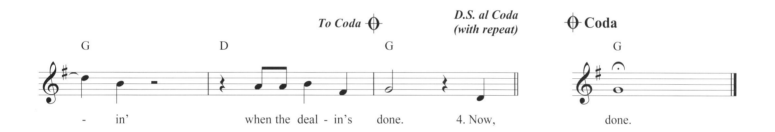

- in' when the deal - in's done. 4. Now,   done.

Additional Lyrics

2. He said, "Son, I've made my life out of readin' people's faces,
   And knowin' what their cards were by the way they held their eyes.
   So, if you don't mind me sayin', I can see you're out of aces.
   For a taste of your whiskey, I'll give you some advice."

3. So, I handed him my bottle and he drank down my last swallow.
   Then he bummed a cigarette and asked me for a light.
   And the night got deathly quiet, and his face lost all expression,
   Said, "If you're gonna play the game, boy, you gotta learn to play it right."

4. Now, ev'ry gambler knows the secret to survivin'
   Is knowin' what to throw away and knowin' what to keep.
   'Cause ev'ry hand's a winner and ev'ry hand's a loser,
   And the best you can hope for is to die in your sleep.

5. So, when he'd finished speakin', he turned back toward the window,
   Crushed out his cigarette and faded off to sleep.
   Then somewhere in the darkness, the gambler, he broke even.
   But in his final words I found an ace that I could keep.

Green Green Grass of Home

Words and Music by Curly Putman

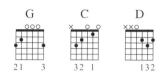

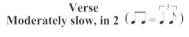

Verse
Moderately slow, in 2

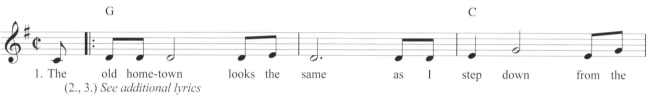

1. The old home-town looks the same as I step down from the
(2., 3.) *See additional lyrics*

train, and there to meet me is my ma - ma and

pa - pa. Down the road I look, and there runs Mar - y,

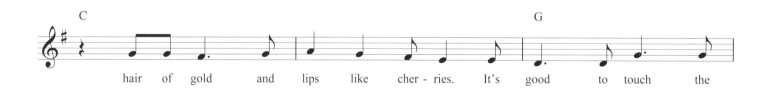

hair of gold and lips like cher - ries. It's good to touch the

green, green grass ___ of home. _____ {(1., 2.) Yes, they'll
{(3.) Yes, they'll

Chorus

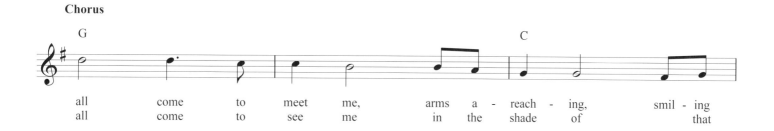

all come to meet me, arms a - reach - ing, smil - ing
all come to see me in the shade of that

sweet - ly. It's good to touch the green, green grass ___ of
old oak tree as they lay me 'neath the green, green grass ___ of

1., 2.   3.

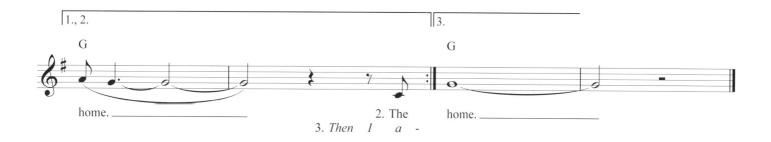

home. _____   2. The   home. _____
3. *Then I a -*

Additional Lyrics

2. The old house is still standing, though the paint is cracked and dry.
And there's that old oak tree that I used to play on.
Down the lane I walk with my sweet Mary, hair of gold and lips like cherries.
It's good to touch the green, green grass of home.

3. *(Spoken:) Then I awake, and look around me at four gray walls that surround me,*
And I realize that I was only dreaming.
For there's a guard and there's a sad, old padre. Arm in arm we'll walk at daybreak.
Again I'll touch the green, green grass of home.

Heartaches by the Number

Words and Music by Harlan Howard

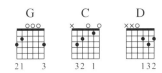

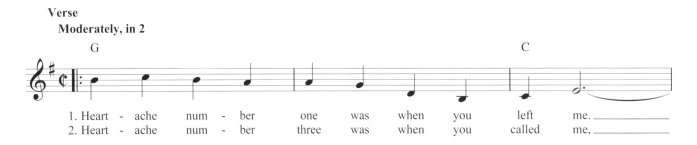

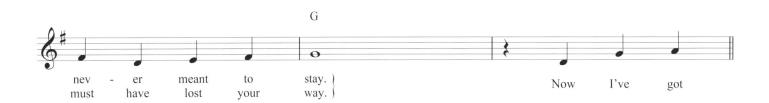

Chorus

heart - aches   by   the   num - ber,   trou - bles   by   the

score.   Ev - 'ry   day   you   love   me   less,   each

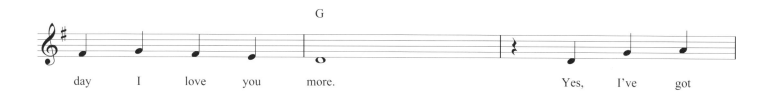

day   I   love   you   more.   Yes,   I've   got

heart - aches   by   the   num - ber, _____   a   love   that   I   can't

win.   But   the   day   that   I   stop   count - ing,   that's   the

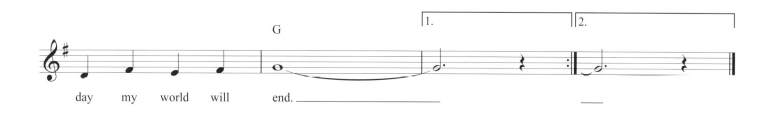

day   my   world   will   end. _____

Hickory Wind

Words and Music by Gram Parsons and Bob Buchanan

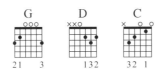

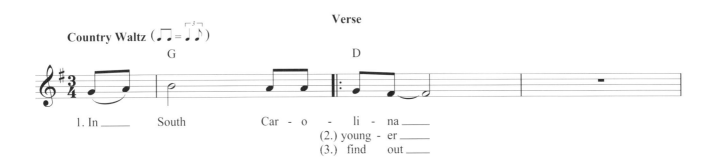

1. In _____ South Car - o - li - na _____
(2.) young - er _____
(3.) find out _____

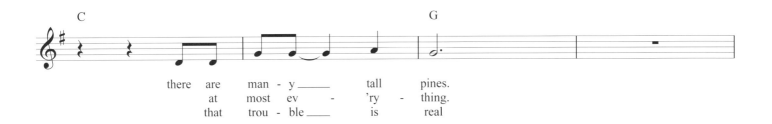

there are man - y _____ tall pines.
at most ev - 'ry - thing.
that trou - ble _____ is real

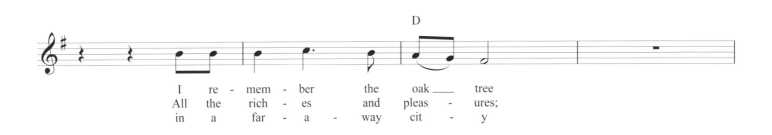

I re - mem - ber the oak _____ tree
All the rich - es and pleas - ures;
in a far - a - way cit - y

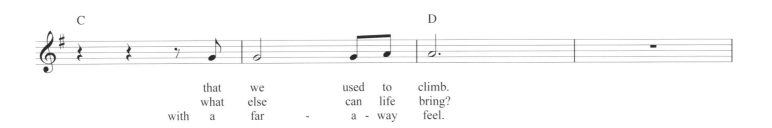

that we used to climb.
what else can life bring?
with a far - a - way feel.

But now when I'm lone - some, _____
But it makes me feel bet - ter _____
But it makes me feel bet - ter _____

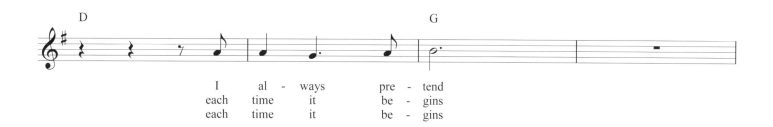

I al - ways pre - tend
each time it be - gins
each time it be - gins

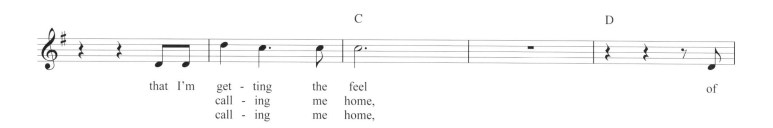

that I'm get - ting the feel of
call - ing me home,
call - ing me home,

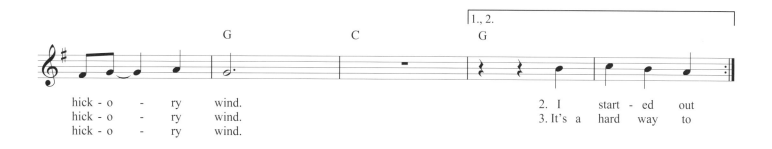

1., 2.

hick - o - ry wind.
hick - o - ry wind.
hick - o - ry wind.

2. I start - ed out
3. It's a hard way to

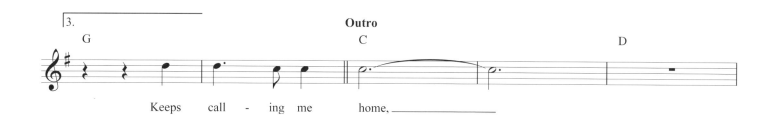

3.

Outro

Keeps call - ing me home, _____

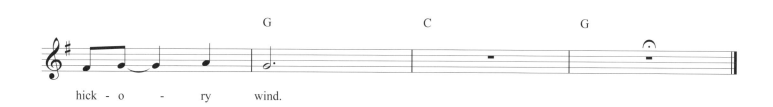

hick - o - ry wind.

Hot Legs

Words and Music by Rod Stewart

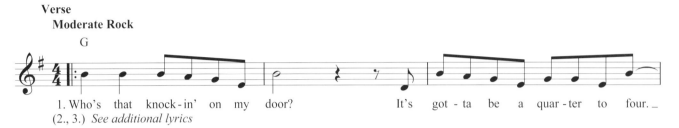

Verse
Moderate Rock

1. Who's that knock-in' on my door? It's got-ta be a quar-ter to four.
(2., 3.) *See additional lyrics*

Is it you __ a-gain, __ com-in' 'round for more? __

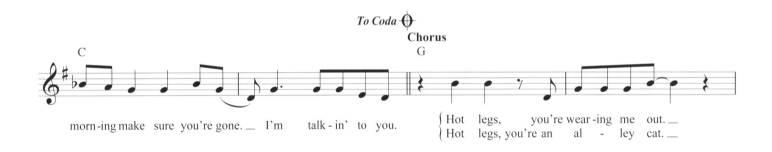

Well, you can love me to-night __ if you want, __ but in the

To Coda ⊕
Chorus

morn-ing make sure you're gone. __ I'm talk-in' to you.

(Hot legs, you're wear-ing me out. __
(Hot legs, you're an al - ley cat. __

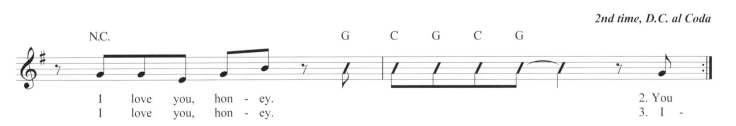

Hot legs, you can scream and shout. __
Hot legs, you scratch my back. __

Hot legs, are you still in school? __
Hot legs, bring your moth-er, too. ___

2nd time, D.C. al Coda

N.C.   G   C   G   C   G

I love you, hon - ey.   2. You
I love you, hon - ey.   3. I -

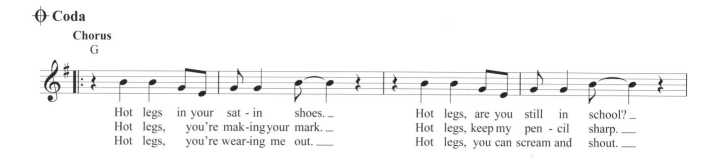

Coda

Chorus

Hot legs in your sat - in shoes. _   Hot legs, are you still in school? _
Hot legs, you're mak-ing your mark. _   Hot legs, keep my pen - cil sharp. __
Hot legs, you're wear-ing me out. __   Hot legs, you can scream and shout. __

Hot legs, you're mak - in' me a fool. _   I love you, hon - ey.
Hot legs, keep your hands to your - self. __   I love you, hon - ey.
Hot legs, you're still in school. _

Outro

I love you, hon - ey.   Hot legs.

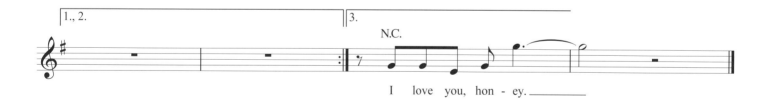

Hot legs.   Hot legs.

I love you, hon - ey. ___

Additional Lyrics

2. You got a most persuasive tongue; you promise all kinds of fun.
 But what you don't understand, I'm a workin' man.
 I'm gonna need a shot of vitamin E by the time you're finished with me.
 I'm talkin' to you.

3. Imagine how my daddy felt in your jet-black suspender belt.
 Seventeen years old, he's trudging sixty-four.
 You got legs right up to your neck. You're making me a physical wreck.
 I'm talkin' to you.

I Feel Lucky

Words and Music by Mary Chapin Carpenter and Don Schlitz

Verse

Moderately

1. Well, I woke up this morn - ing, stum-bled out of my rack. I o - pened up the pa-per to the
(2.) *See additional lyrics*

page in the back. It on - ly took a min - ute for my fin - ger to find ___ my dai -

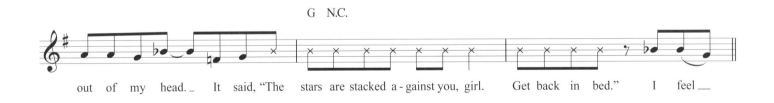

- ly dose of des - ti - ny un - der my sign. My eyes just a - bout popped

out of my head. ___ It said, "The stars are stacked a - gainst you, girl. Get back in bed." I feel ___

Chorus

luck - y,   I feel ___ luck - y, ___ yeah. ___ { No ___
{ No trop -

Pro-fes-sor Doom gon-na stand in my way. __
- i-cal de-pres-sion gon-na steal my sun a-way.)

Mm, __ I feel __ luck-y to-day. _____

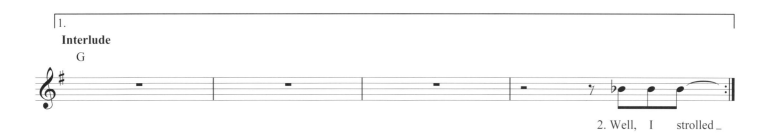

1.

Interlude

G

2. Well, I strolled __

2.

Interlude

C   G

D   G   D

3. Now, e - lev -

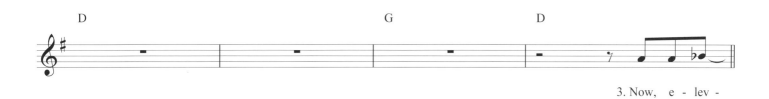

Verse

G N.C.   G N.C.

- en mil-lion lat-er, I was sit-tin' at the bar. I bought __ the house a dou-ble, then the

C

wait-ress a new car. __ Dwight Yoa-kam's in the cor-ner, tryin' __ to catch my eye. Lyle

G N.C.   D N.C.

Lov-ett's right be-side me with his hand up-on my thigh. Mor - al of this sto-ry, it's

simple but it's true: Hey, the stars ___ might lie, ___ but the num-bers nev-er do. I feel

Chorus

luck-y.   Oh, ___ oh, ___ oh, ___ I feel ___ luck-y, _____ yeah. ___   Hey Dwight, _

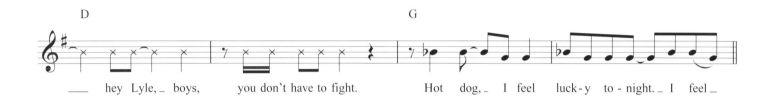

___ hey Lyle, _ boys,   you don't have to fight.   Hot dog, _ I feel luck-y to-night. _ I feel _

Outro-Chorus

luck-y,   I feel _ luck-y, _____ yeah. _   Think I'll flip a coin; _ I'm a

win-ner ei-ther way.   Mm, ___ I feel ___ luck-y to-day. _____

Additional Lyrics

2. Well, I strolled down to the corner, gave my numbers to the clerk.
The pot's eleven million, so I called in sick to work.
I bought a pack of Camels, a burrito and a Barq's,
Crossed against the light, made a beeline for the park.
The sky began to thunder, wind began to moan.
I heard a voice above me sayin',
"Girl, you'd better get back home." But I feel... *(To Chorus)*

I'm So Lonesome I Could Cry

Words and Music by Hank Williams

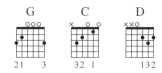

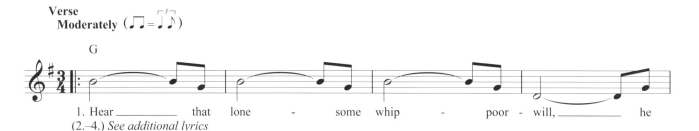

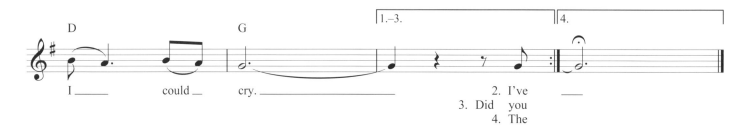

Additional Lyrics

2. I've never seen a night so long,
   When time goes crawling by.
   The moon just went behind a cloud
   To hide its face and cry.

3. Did you ever see a robin weep
   When leaves begin to die?
   That means he's lost the will to live.
   I'm so lonesome I could cry.

4. The silence of a falling star
   Lights up a purple sky.
   And as I wonder where you are,
   I'm so lonesome I could cry.

Route 66

By Bobby Troup

Verse

1. Well, if you ev - er plan __ to mo - tor west, trav - el my __
(2., 3.) *See additional lyrics*

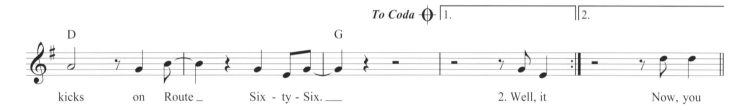

__ way, take the high - way that's the best. Get your

To Coda |1. |2.

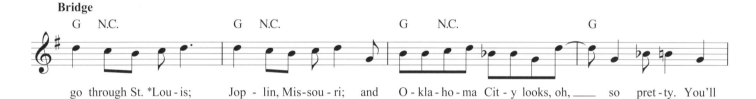

kicks on Route __ Six - ty - Six. __ 2. Well, it Now, you

Bridge

go through St. *Lou - is; Jop - lin, Mis - sou - ri; and O - kla - ho - ma Cit - y looks, oh, __ so pret - ty. You'll

see Am - a - ril - lo; Gal - lup, New Mex - i - co; __ Flag-

D.S. al Coda

- staff, Ar - i - zo - na; don't __ for - get Wi - no - na, King - man, Bar - stow, San __ Ber - nar - di - no. 3. Won't

Coda **Outro** *Repeat and fade*

Get your kicks on Route __ Six - ty - Six. __ Get your

Additional Lyrics

2. Well, it winds from Chicago to L.A.,
   More than two thousand miles all the way.
   Get your kicks on Route Sixty-Six.

3. Won't you get hip to this timely tip
   When you make that California trip?
   Get your kicks on Route Sixty-Six.

*Pronounced "Looey."

Jackson

Words and Music by Billy Edd Wheeler and Jerry Leiber

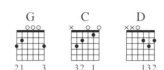

1. We got mar-ried in a fe-ver, hot-ter than a pep-per
(3., 5.) *See additional lyrics*

sprout. We've been talk-in' 'bout Jack-son ev-er since the fire went _

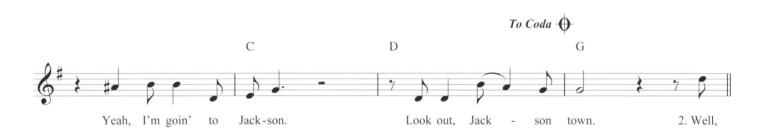

out. _____ I'm goin' to Jack-son, I'm gon-na mess a - round. _

Yeah, I'm goin' to Jack-son. Look out, Jack - son town. 2. Well,

go on down to _ Jack - son. Go a - head and wreck your _ health. Go
(4.) *See additional lyrics*

play your _ hand, you _ big-talk-in' man, and make _ a big fool of _ your -

self. Yeah, go to Jack - son. Go comb your hair.

Hon - ey, I'm gon-na snow-ball Jack - son. See if I care. 3. When

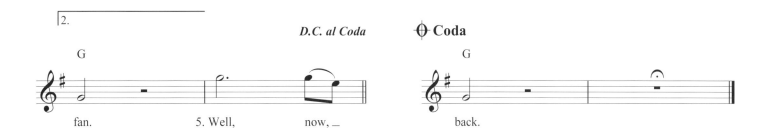

D.C. al Coda   ⊕ **Coda**

fan. 5. Well, now, —   back.

Additional Lyrics

3. When I breeze into that city,
   People gonna stoop and bow.
   All them women gonna make me
   Teach 'em what they don't know how.
   I'm goin' to Jackson.
   You turn loose-a my coat,
   'Cause I'm goin' to Jackson.
   "Goodbye," that's all she wrote.

4. But they'll laugh at you in Jackson,
   And I'll be dancin' on a pony keg.
   They'll lead you 'round town like a scolded hound
   With your tail tucked between your legs.
   Yeah, go to Jackson,
   You big-talkin' man.
   And I'll be waitin' in Jackson,
   Behind my Japan fan.

5. Well, now, we got married in a fever,
   Hotter than a pepper sprout.
   We've been talkin' 'bout Jackson
   Ever since the fire went out.
   I'm goin' to Jackson,
   And that's a fact.
   Yeah, we're goin' to Jackson,
   Ain't never comin' back.

Knock Three Times

Words and Music by Irwin Levine and Larry Russell Brown

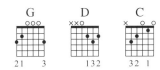

Verse
Moderately

1. Hey, girl, what-cha do - in' down there, danc-in' a - lone ev - 'ry
(2.) you look out your win - dow to - night, pull in the string with the

night while I live right a - bove _____ you? _____
note that's at - tached to my heart. _____

I can hear your mu - sic play - in', _____
Read how man - y times I saw _____ you, _____ how

I can feel your bod - y sway - in'. _____ One floor be - low me, you
in my si - lence I a - dore _____ you, _____ and on - ly in my dreams did

Bridge

haps up - on that lone - ly street, there's some - one such as I

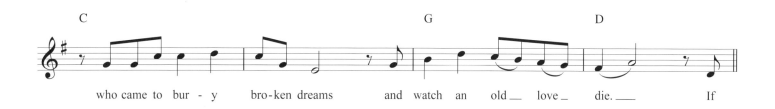

who came to bur - y bro - ken dreams and watch an old love die. If

Outro-Verse

I could find that lone - ly street, where dim lights bring for -

get - ful - ness, where bro - ken dreams and mem - 'ries meet.

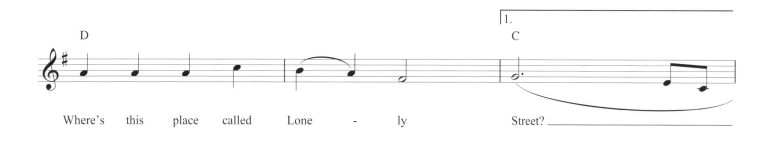

Where's this place called Lone - ly Street?

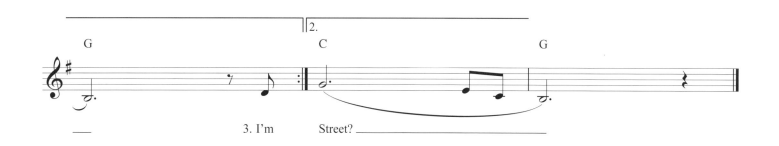

3. I'm Street?

Mammas Don't Let Your Babies Grow Up to Be Cowboys

Words and Music by Ed Bruce and Patsy Bruce

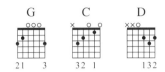

Verse
Moderately fast

1. Cow-boys ain't eas-y to love and they're hard-er to hold.
2. *See additional lyrics*

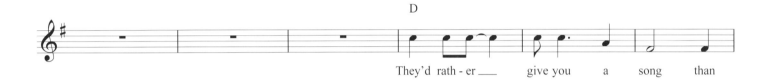

They'd rath-er __ give you a song than

dia-monds or gold. Lone Star belt

buck-les and old fad-ed Le-vis and each night be-gins __ a new day.

If you don't un-der-stand him __ and he don't die young,

he'll prob-'ly just ride __ a-way.

% **Chorus**

Mam - mas, _____ don't let your ba - bies grow up to be _____ cow - boys.

Don't let 'em pick gui - tars and drive them old trucks. Let 'em be doc - tors and law - yers and such.

Mam - mas, _____ don't let your ba - bies grow up to be _____ cow - boys,

'cause they'll nev - er stay home and they're al - ways a - lone, _____ e - ven with some - one they love. _____

To Coda ⊕

⊕ **Coda**

2nd time, D.S. al Coda

love. _____

Additional Lyrics

2. Cowboys like smoky old poolrooms and clear mountain mornings,
Little warm puppies and children, and girls of the night.
Them that don't know him won't like him,
And them that do sometimes won't know how to take him.
He ain't wrong, he's just different,
But his pride won't let him do things to make you think he's right.

Me and Bobby McGee

Words and Music by Kris Kristofferson and Fred Foster

Verse
Moderately, in 2

1. Bust - ed flat __ in Bat - on Rouge,   wait - in' for a train, __   when I's
2. *See additional lyrics*

feel - in' near __ as fad - ed as _____ my _____ jeans.

Bob - by thumbed __ a die - sel down __   just be - fore __ it

rained __   that rode us all __ the way to New Or - leans.   I

pulled my har - poon __ out of my dirt - y red ban - dan - na.   I's

play - in' soft while Bob - by sang the blues, __   yeah. _____

Wind - shield wip - ers slap - pin' time, I's __ hold - in' Bob - by's hand in mine.

We sang ev - 'ry song ___ that driv - er knew. ___

Chorus

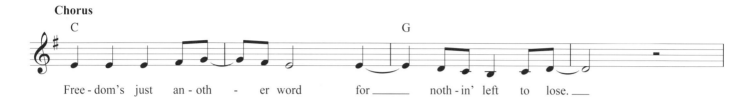

Free - dom's just an - oth - er word for ____ noth - in' left to lose. ___

Noth - in', don't mean noth - in', hon', if it ain't free. ____
Noth - in', that's all ____ that Bob - by left ___ me. ____

If

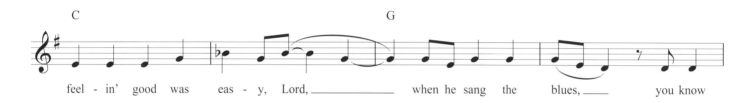

feel - in' good was eas - y, Lord, _____ when he sang the blues, ____ you know

feel - in' good was good e - nough ___ for me, ____

good e - nough ___ for me and my Bob - by Mc - Gee.

Outro

Hey, hey, hey, Bob - by Mc - Gee, ___ yeah. ___

Additional Lyrics

2. From the Kentucky coal mine to the California sun,
   Hey, Bobby shared the secrets of my soul.
   Through all kinds of weather, through ev'rything we done,
   Yeah, Bobby, baby, kept me from the cold.
   One day up near Salinas, Lord, I let him slip away.
   He's lookin' for that home, and I hope he finds it.
   But I'd trade all of my tomorrows for one single yesterday,
   To be holdin' Bobby's body next to mine.

Midnight Special

Words and Music by John Fogerty

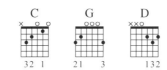

Verse

Moderately

1. Well, you wake up in the morn - ing; you hear the work bell ring.
(2., 3.) *See additional lyrics*

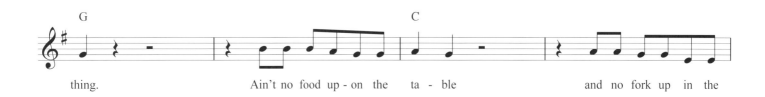

And they march you to the ta - ble to see the same _ old _

thing. Ain't no food up - on the ta - ble and no fork up in the

pan. But you bet - ter not com - plain, boy;

you get in trou - ble with the man. Let the mid - night spe -

Chorus

- cial shine a light on me. _____

Let the mid-night spe - cial shine a light on ___ me. _

___ Let the mid-night spe - cial

shine a light on me. ___ Let the mid-night spe -

To Coda ⊕

- cial shine a ev - er lov - in' light on ___ me. _

1.

2.

D.S. al Coda

⊕ **Coda**

2. Yon - der come Miss Ros -   3. If you're ev - er in   light on ___ me. _

Additional Lyrics

2. Yonder come Miss Rosie.
   How in the world did you know?
   By the way she wears her apron
   And the clothes she wore.
   Umbrella on her shoulder,
   Piece of paper in the hand.
   She come to see the Governor;
   She wants to free her man.

3. If you're ever in Houston,
   Well, you better do right.
   You better not gamble,
   You better not fight,
   Or the sheriff will grab ya,
   And the boys will bring you down.
   The next thing you know, boy,
   Oh, you're prison-bound.

Nadine
(Is It You)

Words and Music by Chuck Berry

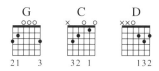

Verse
Moderately fast

1. As I got on a cit-y bus and found a va-cant seat, I
(2.–4.) *See additional lyrics*

thought I saw my fu-ture bride _ walk-ing up the street. I shout-ed to the driv-er, "Hey, con-

duc-tor, you must _ slow down. _ I think I see her; please let me off the bus." Na-dine, _

Chorus

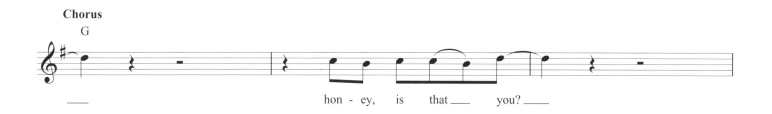

_ hon-ey, is that _ you? _

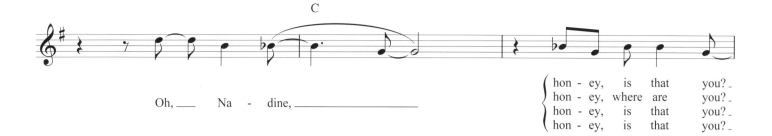

Oh, ___ Na - dine, ___

hon - ey, is that you? _
hon - ey, where are you? _
hon - ey, is that you? _
hon - ey, is that you? _

___
___
___
___

Seem like ev - 'ry time I see you, dar - lin',
Seem like ev - 'ry time I catch up with you,
Seem like ev - 'ry time I catch up with you,
Seem like ev - 'ry time I see you, dar - lin',

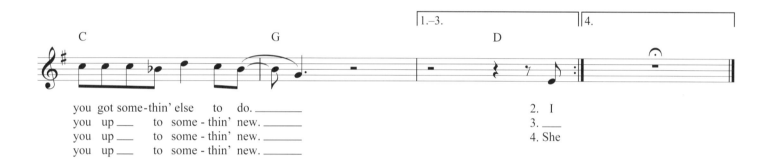

1.–3.   4.

you got some - thin' else to do. _____
you up ___ to some - thin' new. _____
you up ___ to some - thin' new. _____
you up ___ to some - thin' new. _____

2. I
3. ___
4. She

Additional Lyrics

2. I saw her from the corner when she turned and doubled back,
And she started walkin' toward a coffee-colored Cadillac.
I was pushin' through the crowd, tryin' to get where she was at,
And I was campaign shoutin' like a Southern diplomat.

3. Downtown searchin' for her, lookin' all around.
Saw her getting in a yellow cab, headin' uptown.
I caught a loaded taxi, paid up everybody's tab,
Flipped a twenty-dollar bill and told him, "Catch that yellow cab."

4. She moves around like a wayward summer breeze.
Go, driver, go. Go catch her for me, please.
Movin' through the traffic like a mounted cavalier,
Leanin' out the taxi window, tryin' to make her hear.

Old Time Rock & Roll

Words and Music by George Jackson and Thomas E. Jones III

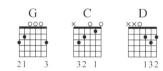

Chorus

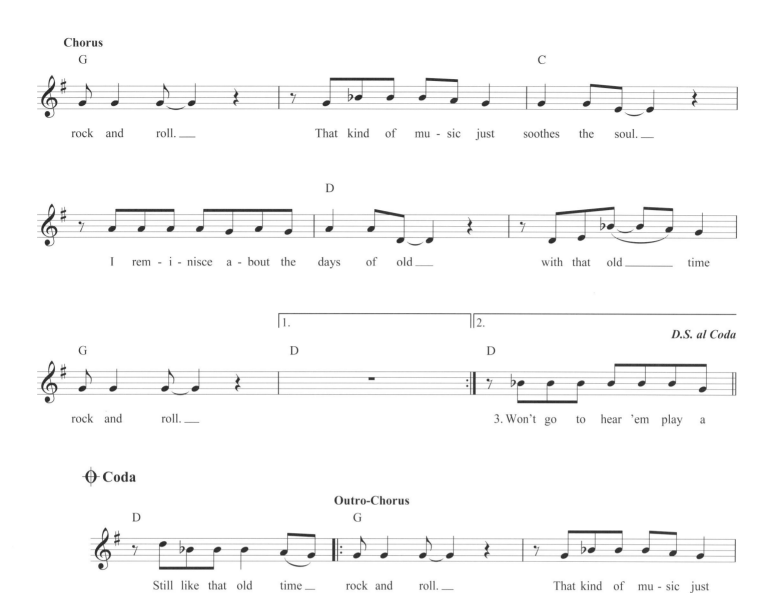

rock and roll. ___ That kind of mu - sic just soothes the soul. ___

I rem - i - nisce a - bout the days of old ___ with that old ___ time

rock and roll. ___ 3. Won't go to hear 'em play a

D.S. al Coda

⊕ Coda

Outro-Chorus

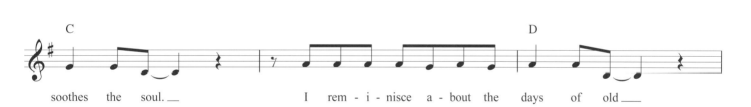

Still like that old time ___ rock and roll. ___ That kind of mu - sic just

soothes the soul. ___ I rem - i - nisce a - bout the days of old ___

Repeat and fade

with that old ___ time rock and roll. ___ Still like that old time ___

Additional Lyrics

3. Won't go to hear 'em play a tango.
   I'd rather hear some blues or funky old soul.
   There's only one sure way to get me to go:
   Start playin' old time rock and roll.
   Call me a relic, call me what you will.
   Say I'm old-fashioned, say I'm over the hill.
   Today's music ain't got the same soul.
   I like that old time rock and roll.

Party Doll

Words and Music by James Bowen and Buddy Knox

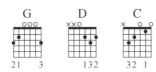

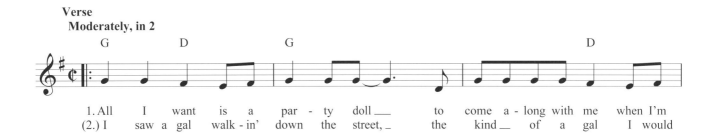

1. All I want is a par-ty doll ___ to come a-long with me when I'm
(2.) I saw a gal walk-in' down the street, ___ the kind ___ of a gal I would

feel - in' wild, ___ to be ev - er lov - in' and
love to meet. ___ She had blonde ___ hair and ___

true and fair, ___ to run her ___ fin - gers a - through my hair.
eyes of blue. ___ Ba - by, I'm a - gon - na have a par - ty with you.

Come a - long and be my par - ty doll. ___ Come a - long and be my
par - ty doll. ___ Come a - long and be my par - ty doll. ___

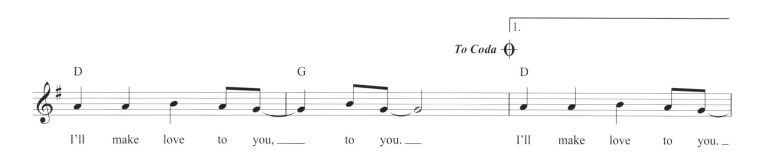

To Coda ⊕

I'll make love to you, ____ to you. ____ I'll make love to you. _

____ 2. Well, I'll make love to you. ____

Bridge

Ev - 'ry man has got - ta have a par - ty doll ____ to be with him ____ when he's

feel - in' wild, ____ to be ev - er lov - in', true and fair, ____ to

run her fin - gers through his hair, ____ to run her fin - gers

⊕ **Coda**

D.S. al Coda

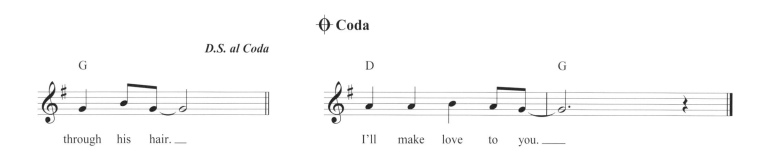

through his hair. ____

I'll make love to you. ____

Ready Teddy

Words and Music by John Marascalco and Robert Blackwell

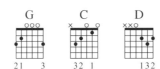

Ready, set, go, man, go. I've got a gal that I love so. I'm

ready, ready, ready Teddy. I'm read-y, ready, ready Teddy. I'm read-

-y, ready, ready Teddy. I'm ready, ready, ready to rock 'n' roll.

1. Goin' to the corner, pick up my sweetie pie. She's my rock 'n' roll baby, she's the apple of my eye. I'm

ready, ready, ready Teddy. I'm read-y, ready, ready Teddy. I'm read-

-y, ready, ready Teddy. I'm ready, ready, ready to rock 'n' roll. 2. Now the

Rock Me

Words and Music by John Kay

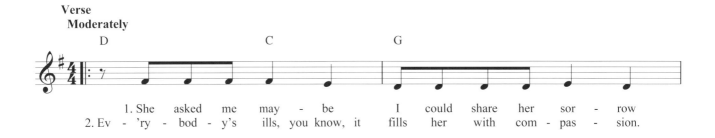

Verse
Moderately

1. She asked me may - be I could share her sor - row
2. Ev - 'ry - bod - y's ills, you know, it fills her with com - pas - sion.

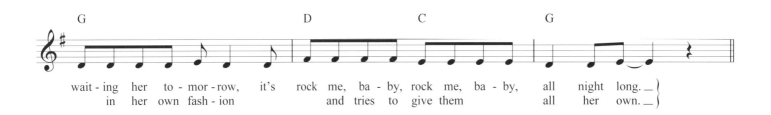

a - bout the men that tried to treat her wrong. 'Tho just a ba - by a-
That's why she tries to save the world a - lone. She helps the need - y

wait - ing her to - mor - row, it's rock me, ba - by, rock me, ba - by, all night long.
in her own fash - ion and tries to give them all her own.

Pre-Chorus

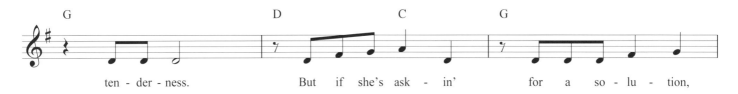

She needs an an - swer to her con - fu - sion, some - one to guide her with

ten - der - ness. But if she's ask - in' for a so - lu - tion,

all that she gets, you know, is some-thing like this: I

Chorus

don't know where we come ___ from, don't know where we're go - in' to. ___

___ But if all this should have a rea - son,

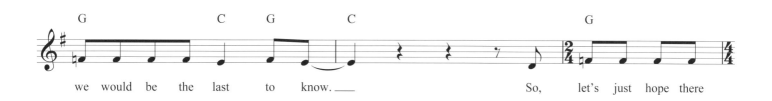

we would be the last to know. ___ So, let's just hope there

1.

is a Prom - ised Land. Hang on till then, ___ as best as you can. ___

2.

Outro *Repeat and fade*

best as you can. ___ Rock me, ba - by, rock me, ba - by, all night long. ___

Sad Songs
(Say So Much)

Words and Music by Elton John and Bernie Taupin

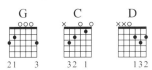

Verse

Moderately

1. Guess there are times ___ when we ___ all ___ need ___ to share ___ a lit - tle pain ___
(2.) suf - fer - in' ___ e - nough, ___ oh, ___ to write ___ it down ___

and iron-ing out the rough spots ___ is the hard - est part when mem - o - ries re-main.
when ev -'ry sin-gle word makes sense, ___ then it's eas - i - er to have those songs a-round.

And it's times ___ like these when we all ___ need ___ to hear ___ the ra - di - o, ___
The kick in - side ___ is in ___ the ___ line ___ that fi - nal-ly gets ___ to you. ___

'cause from the lips ___ of ___ some ___ old sing - er we can share the trou-bles we al-read-y know. }
And it feels so good to hurt ___ so bad ___ and suf-fer just e-nough to sing ___ the blues. ___ }

𝄋 Chorus

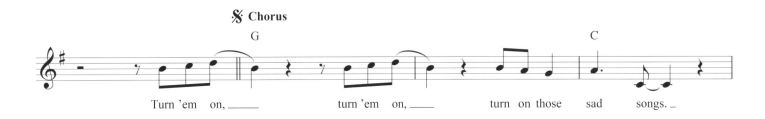

Turn 'em on, ___ turn 'em on, ___ turn on those sad songs.

When all hope is gone, ___ why don't you tune in and turn ___ them on?

They reach in - to your room, oh, _____ just feel _ their _ gen - tle touch. _

To Coda

When all hope is gone, __ a sad song _ says _ so much. _

1. 2.

Bridge

2. If some-one else is   Sad songs, _ they _ say,   sad songs, _ they _

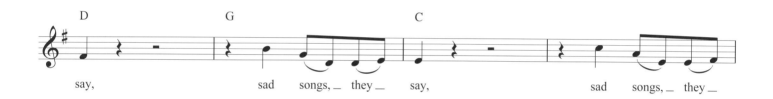

say,   sad songs, _ they _ say,   sad songs, _ they _

D.S. al Coda   **Coda**

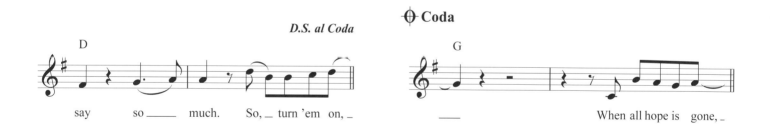

say so _____ much. So, _ turn 'em on, _   ___ When all hope is gone, _

Outro

___ you know a sad song _ says _ so much. _   When ev -'ry lit - tle bit of

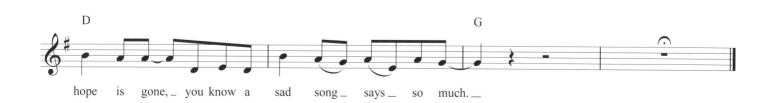

hope is gone, _ you know a sad song _ says _ so much. _

She Don't Know She's Beautiful

Words and Music by Bob McDill and Paul Harrison

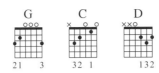

1. We go out ___ to a par - ty some - where. The
2. There she goes, ___ just walk - in' down the street, and
3. Morn - ing comes, ___ her hair's ___ all ___ a mess; that's

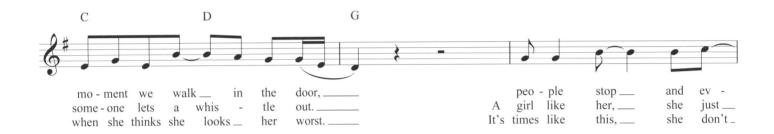

mo - ment we walk ___ in the door, ___ peo - ple stop ___ and ev -
some - one lets a whis - tle out. ___ A girl like her, ___ she just ___
when she thinks she looks ___ her worst. ___ It's times like this, ___ she don't ___

To Coda ⊕

- 'ry - bod - y stares. She don't know what they're star - ing for. ___
___ can't ___ see what the fuss is all a - bout. ___
___ know ___ why I can't take my eyes off her. ___

Chorus

She don't know ___ she's beau - ti - ful. (Nev - er crossed her

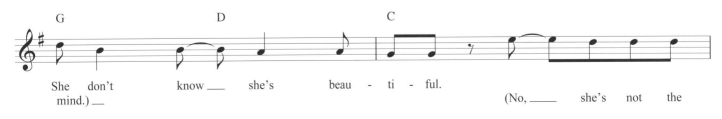

She don't know ___ she's beau - ti - ful.
mind.) ___ (No, ___ she's not the

80

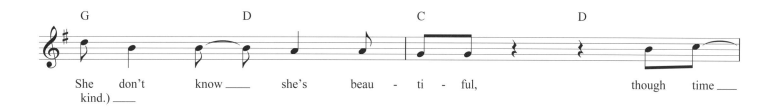

She don't know   she's beau - ti - ful,   though time

kind.)

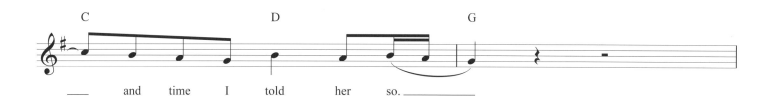

   and time I told her so.

2nd time, D.C. al Coda

 Coda

Outro-Chorus

She don't   know   she's beau - ti - ful. (Nev - er crossed her

She don't   know   she's beau - ti - ful.

mind.)   (No,   she's not the

Repeat and fade

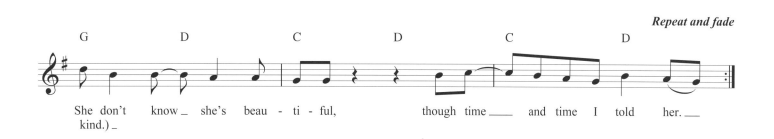

She don't know   she's beau - ti - ful,   though time   and time I told her.

kind.)

Sugar, Sugar

Words and Music by Andy Kim and Jeff Barry

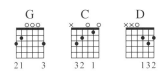

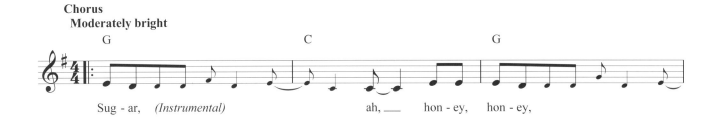

Chorus
Moderately bright

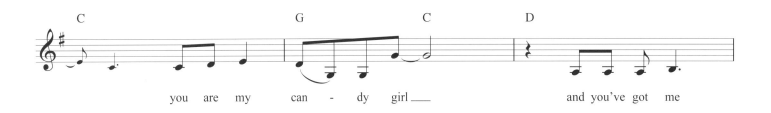

Sug - ar,   *(Instrumental)*   ah, ___ hon - ey, hon - ey,

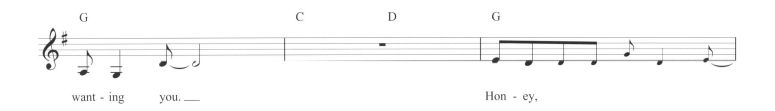

you are my can - dy girl ___ and you've got me

want - ing you. ___   Hon - ey,

ah, ___ sug - ar, sug - ar,   you are my

can - dy girl ___   and you've got me   want - ing you. ___

Verse

1. I just can't be-lieve the love - li - ness of lov - ing you. (I just can't be-lieve it's true.) __
2. When I kissed you, girl, I knew __ how sweet a kiss could be. (I know how sweet a kiss can be.) __

1.

I just can't be - lieve the won - der of this feel - ing, too. (I just can't be - lieve it's true.) __
Like the sum - mer sun - shine, pour __ your sweet - ness o - ver me.

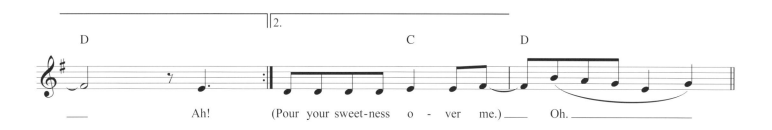

2.

__ Ah! (Pour your sweet - ness o - ver me.) __ Oh. _____

Outro

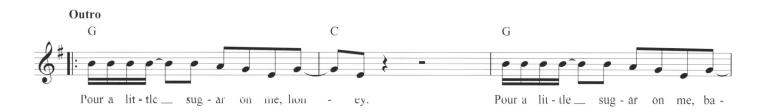

Pour a lit - tle __ sug - ar on me, hon - ey. Pour a lit - tle __ sug - ar on me, ba -

- by. I'm gon - na make your life __ so sweet, yeah, yeah, __ yeah.

1. 2. *D.C. and fade*

Pour a lit - tle __ sug - ar on me. Oh, yeah. __ Pour a lit - tle __ sug - ar on me, hon - ey. Ah!

83

Time for Me to Fly

Words and Music by Kevin Cronin

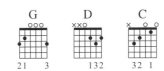

Verse
Moderately, in 2

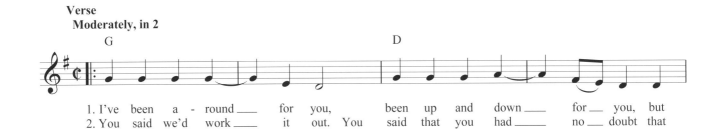

1. I've been a-round ___ for you, been up and down ___ for ___ you, but
2. You said we'd work ___ it out. You said that you had ___ no ___ doubt that

I just can't get an-y re-lief. ___ I've
deep down we were real-ly in love. ___ But

swal-lowed my pride ___ for you, lived and lied ___ for ___ you, but
I'm tired of hold-ing on to a feel-ing I know ___ is ___ gone. I

you still make me feel like a thief. ___ You got me
do be-lieve that I've had e-nough. ___ I've had e -

Chorus

steal-in' your love ___ a-way 'cause you nev-er give ___ it,
nough of the false-ness of a worn-out re-la-tion, e -

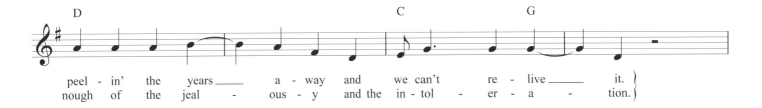

peel-in' the years ___ a-way and we can't re-live ___ it. }
nough of the jeal-ous-y and the in-tol-er-a-tion. }

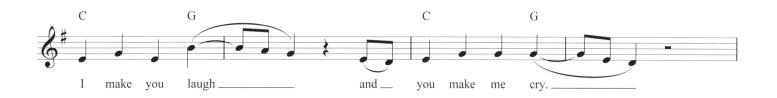

I make you laugh _____ and _ you make me cry. _____

I be-lieve it's time _ for me _ to fly. _____

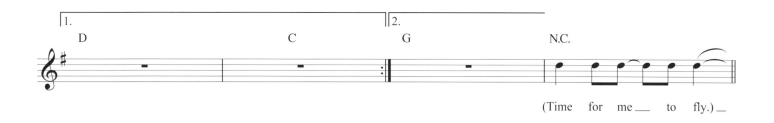

(Time for me _ to fly.) _

Outro

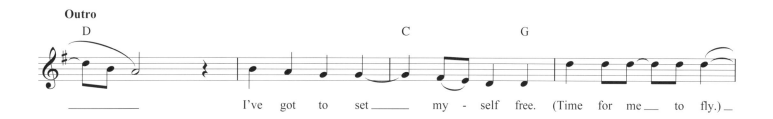

_____ I've got to set _____ my - self free. (Time for me _ to fly.) _

_____ That's just how it's got to _ be. _____

I know it hurts to say _ good - bye, _____ but it's time for me _ to fly. _____

It's time for me _ to fly. _____

T-R-O-U-B-L-E

Words and Music by Jerry Chesnut

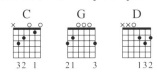

Verse

lit - tle bit - ty ba - by when my pa - pa hit the skids. Ma - ma had a time tryin' to raise nine kids.
(3., 4.) *See additional lyrics*

Told me not to stare 'cause it was im - po - lite, _ and did the best she could to try to raise me right. _ But

Ma - ma nev - er told me 'bout - a noth - in' like - a Y - O - U. _____ Say, your

moth - er must - 've been an - oth - er some - thin' or an - oth - er, too. _____ Say,

hey, good L - dou - ble - O - K - I - N - G, _____

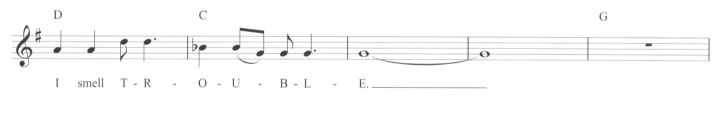

I smell T - R - O - U - B - L - E. _____

Outro   *Repeat and fade*

3., 4. Well, you talk _   Hey, hey, hey. _____   Hey, hey, hey. _____   Hey, hey, hey. _

Additonal Lyrics

3. Well, you talk about a woman, I've seen a lotta others
   With too much somethin' and not enough of another,
   You've got it all together like a lovin' machine,
   Lookin' like glory and walkin' like a dream.
   Mother Nature's sure been good to Y-O-U.
   Well, your mother must've been another good lookin' mother, too.
   Say, hey, good L-double-O-K-I-N-G, I smell T-R-O-U-B-L-E.

4. Well, you talk about a trouble-makin' hunka' pokey bait
   The men are gonna love and all the women gonna hate.
   Remindin' them of everything they're never gonna be,
   Maybe the beginnin' of World War Three.
   'Cause the world ain't ready for nothing like-a Y-O-U.
   I bet your mother must've been another somethin' or the other, too.
   Say, hey, good L-double O-K-I-N-G, I smell T-R-O-U-B-L-E.

Up Around the Bend

Words and Music by John Fogerty

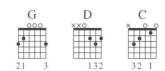

Verse
Moderately

1. There's a place up a-head and I'm goin' just as fast as my feet can fly.
2.–4. *See additional lyrics*

Come a-way, come a-way if you're go - in', leave the sink - in' ship be - hind.

Chorus

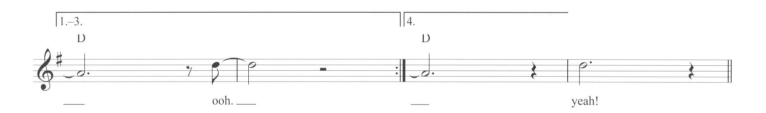

Come on the ris - in' wind. We're go - in' up a - round the bend,

1.–3. ooh.

4. yeah!

Outro

Repeat and fade

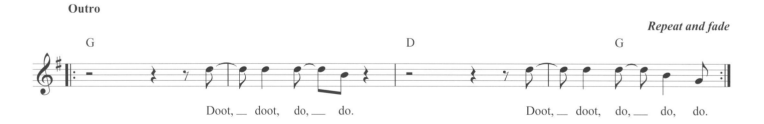

Doot, doot, do, do. Doot, doot, do, do, do.

Additional Lyrics

2. Bring a song and a smile for the banjo.
   Better get while the gettin's good.
   Hitch a ride to end of the highway
   Where the neons turn to wood.

3. You can ponder perpetual motion,
   Fix your mind on a crystal day.
   Always time for a good conversation,
   There's an ear for what you say.

4. Catch a ride to the end of the highway
   And we'll meet by the big red tree.
   There's a place up ahead and I'm goin'.
   Come along, come along with me.

Willie and the Hand Jive

Words and Music by Johnny Otis

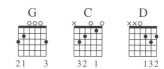

Verse
Moderately, in 2

1. I know a cat named Way-Out Wil-lie.
2.–5. *See additional lyrics*

He got a

cool lit-tle chick called Rock-in' Mil-lie. He can walk and stroll and Su-sie Q, —

and do that cra-zy Hand Jive, too. _ Hand

Chorus

Jive.   Hand   Jive.   Hand   Jive.

1.–4.   5.

Do-in' that cra-zy Hand   Jive.

Additional Lyrics

2. Papa told Willie, "You'll ruin my home.
   You and that Hand Jive has got to go."
   Willie said, "Papa don't put me down.
   They're doin' the Hand Jive all over town."

3. Mama, Mama, look at Uncle Joe.
   He's doin' the Hand Jive with sister Flo.
   Grandma gave baby sister a dime,
   Said, "Do that Hand Jive one more time."

4. Doctor and a lawyer and an Indian chief,
   Now they all dig that crazy beat.
   Way-Out Willie gave 'em all a treat
   When he did that Hand Jive with his feet.

5. Willie and Millie got married last fall.
   They had a little Willie Jr. and that ain't all.
   Well, the baby got famous in his crib, you see,
   Doin' the Hand Jive on TV.

When You Say Nothing at All

Words and Music by Don Schlitz and Paul Overstreet

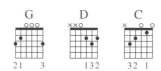

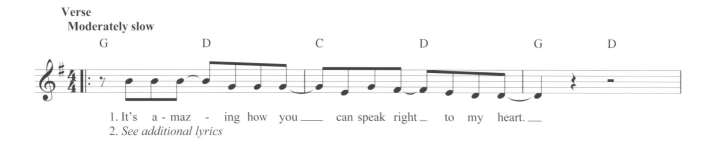

Verse
Moderately slow

1. It's a - maz - ing how you ___ can speak right ___ to my heart. ___
2. *See additional lyrics*

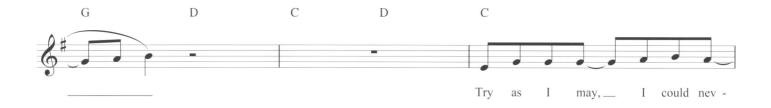

With - out say - ing a word, ___ you can light up the dark. ___

Try as I may, ___ I could nev -

- er ex - plain ___ what I hear ___ when you don't ___ say a thing. ___ The

𝄋 Chorus

smile on your face ___ lets me know ___ that you need ___ me. There's a truth in your eyes ___ say - ing you'll

___ nev-er leave ___ me.   A touch of your hand ___ says you'll catch ___ me if ev - er I fall. ___

1.

To Coda ⊕

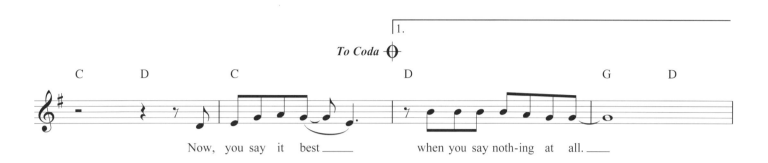
Now, you say it best ___   when you say noth-ing at all. ___

2.

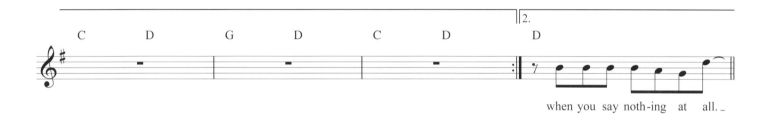
when you say noth-ing at all. _

Interlude

D.S. al Coda

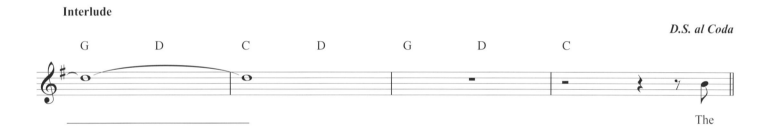
The

⊕ **Coda**

Outro

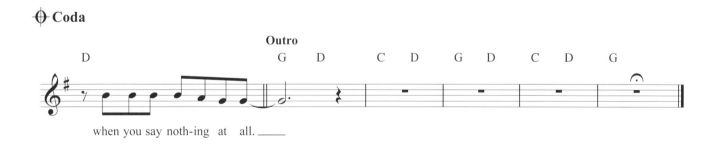
when you say noth-ing at all. ___

Additional Lyrics

2. All day long I can hear people talking out loud.
But when you hold me near, you drown out the crowd.
Old Mister Webster could never define
What's being said between your heart and mine.

Your Mama Don't Dance

Words and Music by Jim Messina and Kenny Loggins

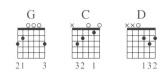

Your ma-ma don't dance and your dad-dy don't rock and roll. ___

Your ma-ma don't dance and your dad-dy don't rock and roll. _

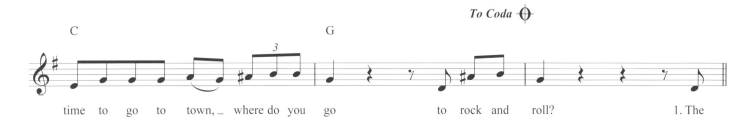

When eve-ning rolls a-round and it's

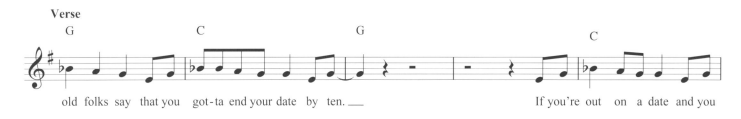

time to go to town, _ where do you go to rock and roll? 1. The

old folks say that you got-ta end your date by ten. ___ If you're out on a date and you

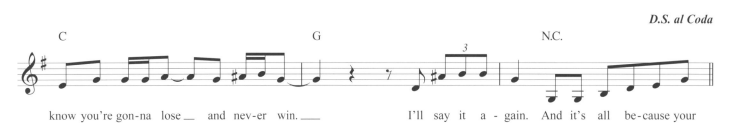

bring her home late, it's a sin. There just ain't no ex-cuse and you

C   G   N.C.

know you're gon-na lose _ and nev-er win. ___ I'll say it a-gain. And it's all be-cause your

Guitar Chord Songbooks

Each 6" x 9" book includes complete lyrics, chord symbols, and guitar chord diagrams.

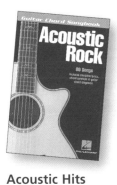 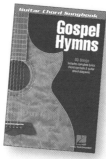 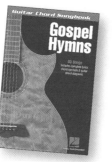 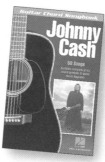 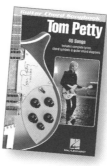

Acoustic Hits
00701787 . . . . $14.99

Acoustic Rock
00699540 . . . . $19.99

Alabama
00699914 . . . . $14.95

The Beach Boys
00699566 . . . . $15.99

The Beatles (A-I)
00699558 . . . . $17.99

The Beatles (J-Y)
00699562 . . . . $17.99

Bluegrass
00702585 . . . . $14.99

Johnny Cash
00699648 . . . . $17.99

Children's Songs
00699539 . . . . $16.99

Christmas Carols
00699536 . . . . $12.99

Christmas Songs – 2nd Edition
00119911 . . . . $14.99

Eric Clapton
00699567 . . . . $16.99

Classic Rock
00699598 . . . . $16.99

Coffeehouse Hits
00703318 . . . . $14.99

Country
00699534 . . . . $14.99

Country Favorites
00700609 . . . . $14.99

Country Hits
00140859 . . . . $14.99

Country Standards
00700608 . . . . $12.95

Cowboy Songs
00699636 . . . . $14.99

Creedence Clearwater Revival
00701786 . . . . $15.99

Jim Croce
00148087 . . . . $14.99

Crosby, Stills & Nash
00701609 . . . . $12.99

John Denver
02501697 . . . . $16.99

Neil Diamond
00700606 . . . . $17.99

Disney
00701071 . . . . $16.99

The Best of Bob Dylan
14037617 . . . . $17.99

Eagles
00122917 . . . . $16.99

Early Rock
00699916 . . . . $14.99

Folksongs
00699541 . . . . $14.99

Folk Pop Rock
00699651 . . . . $15.99

40 Easy Strumming Songs
00115972 . . . . $14.99

Four Chord Songs
00701611 . . . . $14.99

Glee
00702501 . . . . $14.99

Gospel Hymns
00700463 . . . . $14.99

Grand Ole Opry®
00699885 . . . . $16.95

Grateful Dead
00139461 . . . . $14.99

Green Day
00103074 . . . . $14.99

Guitar Chord Songbook White Pages
00702609 . . . . $29.99

Irish Songs
00701044 . . . . $14.99

Michael Jackson
00137847 . . . . $14.99

Billy Joel
00699632 . . . . $16.99

Elton John
00699732 . . . . $15.99

Ray LaMontagne
00130337 . . . . $12.99

Latin Songs
00700973 . . . . $14.99

Love Songs
00701043 . . . . $14.99

Bob Marley
00701704 . . . . $14.99

Bruno Mars
00125332 . . . . $12.99

Paul McCartney
00385035 . . . . $16.95

Steve Miller
00701146 . . . . $12.99

Modern Worship
00701801 . . . . $16.99

Motown
00699734 . . . . $17.99

Willie Nelson
00148273 . . . . $14.99

Nirvana
00699762 . . . . $16.99

Roy Orbison
00699752 . . . . $16.99

Peter, Paul & Mary
00103013 . . . . $14.99

Tom Petty
00699883 . . . . $15.99

Pink Floyd
00139116 . . . . $14.99

Pop/Rock
00699538 . . . . $16.99

Praise & Worship
00699634 . . . . $14.99

Elvis Presley
00699633 . . . . $15.99

Queen
00702395 . . . . $12.99

Red Hot Chili Peppers
00699710 . . . . $17.99

The Rolling Stones
00137716 . . . . $17.99

Bob Seger
00701147 . . . . $12.99

Carly Simon
00121011 . . . . $14.99

Sting
00699921 . . . . $15.99

Taylor Swift
00263755 . . . . $16.99

Three Chord Acoustic Songs
00123860 . . . . $14.99

Three Chord Songs
00699720 . . . . $14.99

Two-Chord Songs
00119236 . . . . $14.99

U2
00137744 . . . . $14.99

Hank Williams
00700607 . . . . $14.99

Stevie Wonder
00120862 . . . . $14.99

Neil Young–Decade
00700464 . . . . $14.99

Visit Hal Leonard online at **www.halleonard.com**